Suffrage sn

Ida Husted Harper

Alpha Editions

This edition published in 2024

ISBN : 9789364738590

Design and Setting By
Alpha Editions
www.alphaedis.com
Email - info@alphaedis.com

As per information held with us this book is in Public Domain. This book is a reproduction of an important historical work. Alpha Editions uses the best technology to reproduce historical work in the same manner it was first published to preserve its original nature. Any marks or number seen are left intentionally to preserve its true form.

SUFFRAGE SNAPSHOTS

By

IDA HUSTED HARPER

These random paragraphs are a few of many which have appeared in *Judge* to express the lighter side of the so-called "woman question." This centers in the suffrage movement but woman's quest of the vote is not a joke. It means a great deal of hard work, many anxious hours, some keen disappointments, yet those who are not in the thick of the fray will never know the good times they have missed. Flashes of fun have been scattered all along the way like flecks of sunshine on a shaded path. It will seem very dull for a little while after the vote is won and women get their rights, but they will soon be able to make things lively again and contribute as always to the gayety of the nation.

Original matter copyrighted by *The Leslie-Judge Publishing Co.* and used in its present form by their courtesy.

Miss Jane Addams in her suffrage speeches insists that men have nothing to fear, for the women will vote right. That very fact gives some of them everything to fear.

Edison says, "the movement for woman suffrage is just plain morals." Maybe that's the trouble—they're too plain. Dress them up fashionably and see if the lady "antis" won't accept them.

A new Chicago policewoman has qualified as one of the best shots on the force, 92 out of 100. Does she vote because she is such a good shot or can she shoot so well because she is a voter? What is the connection between shooting and voting anyway?

Annie Riley Hale, a prominent "anti," says that women want the suffrage in order to establish polygamy throughout the United States. If she can prove it will have that effect the women can take a rest and the men will carry on their campaign for them.

It looks as if one recall, one defeat and then another election had started wings on Mayor Hi Gill, of Seattle. After the tragic close of his first term his chief of police and alleged partner in sinful practices was sent to prison. The women gave Hi another chance and now he has appointed as chief of police the ministers' candidate for mayor and is trying to live up to his chief's standard. Meanwhile the women are standing by with their spectacles on and a recall petition handy.

If Mr. Bryan writes the next Democratic platform it is safe to wager there will be one plank in it which he flatly refused to put in the last one.

Why don't the "antis" get a sewing society somewhere to pass a resolution against woman suffrage? It is growing terribly monotonous to have all the women's organizations in the country declaring in favor.

It is said the Ohio Board of Administration is appalled at the number of imbeciles in the State. We thought there must be quite a lot of them when 528,295 votes were cast against the woman-suffrage amendment recently.

Women have voted for over twenty years in Colorado and twenty-one judges of districts courts have sent letters to United States Senator Shafroth, testifying that they never have known a case of divorce because of political differences between husband and wife. Another anti-suffrage bomb failed to explode!

Dear, dear, how times have changed! Once a woman was not considered a person by law and a wife and husband were one and he was it. Now the highest court in New York has decided that a wife is not only a person and an individual in her own right but she is a family! "A childless widow or a deserted wife without children is included in the term family"—those are the very words. From nobody to a whole family—what an evolution!

A Chicago girl swam two miles to shore from an overturned boat, dragging her escort who couldn't swim. Now the delicate question arises, Which shall do the proposing?

The High Court of Great Britain has decided that a woman cannot practice law because she is not a "person;" but she can be a Queen because a Queen does not have to be a person—at least that is all anybody can make out of the decision.

Mr. Hugh Fox, secretary of the United States Brewers' Association, assures the women that it will make no organized opposition to the pending suffrage amendments. Maybe not—but there is something mightily suggestive in that name.

"Tariff reform, fiscal policies, large international relations are foreign to the consciousness of the average woman," says Mrs. Dodge, president of the anti-suffragists. Maybe so, but it seems as if she might have sense enough to put a mark on a ballot opposite an eagle, a star or a moose's head.

A man was excused from serving as juror in a murder trial in New York lately because his wife wouldn't allow him to convict any one of murder. Out in Oregon a juror was challenged the other day because his wife had already been accepted and it would be impossible for him to give an unbiased opinion. What makes people think that under equal suffrage wives would all vote as their husbands do?

The women voters of Arizona have started in on so many reforms that the men can almost feel their wings sprouting.

The president of the New York State "antis" says, "Suffrage is going, not coming." Well, it sure does seem to be going some these days.

It seems as if, when not only State courts but the United States government itself forbids the use of aigrettes, women would give up trying to wear them; but the Injun in 'em dies hard.

A French naturalist has discovered that the female oyster is far more palatable than the male. This is the case with all animals that are used for food. It is a common remark about a woman that she looks good enough to eat, but did anybody ever say that about a man?

It seems as if the suffragists have come not to bring peace but a sword into the world. When Mrs. Chapman Catt, the international president, was sailing across the Pacific homeward from her little trip to organize the world for woman suffrage, all was calm and serene until she was called on for a speech. "Before this," said one of the men voyagers, "we were all at peace with one another; but after that woman spoke, everybody was fighting over the suffrage question." This is a hint to hostesses: When your guests seem bored to extinction, just get somebody to say woman suffrage, and then watch the sparks fly!

It is said that in England whiskers are again to be the style. One thing is certain—if they become the fashion in this country, our women will set their faces against them!

The dress skirt this fall is to be narrower than ever, and a noted tailor says the only question is, "Can a lady wear it?" Perhaps a lady can, but a modest woman won't.

And now they say President Wilson is about to reverse his position on amending the Sherman anti-trust law. When he gets ready to back track on the woman-suffrage question he will have no difficulty in establishing a precedent.

In the debate in the North Carolina senate on a bill to permit women to act as notaries public it was objected to because women write a "vertical hand" and wear slit skirts. That shouldn't disqualify them as notaries, but it is as strong an argument against giving them the suffrage as one often hears.

The New York City board of education dismissed a woman fireman from one of the public schools, on the ground that it was not suitable work for a woman. It's all right for her to get up at home winter mornings and make the fire but whenever there is a salary attached the work becomes unwomanly. Strange that women cannot see these things without having to be shown so often. There ought to be little sign-boards set up along their path, saying, "Public salaries are only for voters."

"Yeast," a new suffrage play, is just being tried out. It is sure to cause a rise among the "antis."

A bill is before Congress to annex the North Pole as United States territory. Bet it comes in with a Votes for Women flag on the end of it.

If the suffragists and the "antis" don't quit writing letters to members of Congress the latter will raise the rate of postage instead of lowering it.

Recent census reports show that 86.7 of all persons over twenty-five marry. That is quite enough—the other 13.3 are needed to show the married what they escaped.

The woman-suffrage question in this country has been settled. The Colonel did it in his whirlwind tour of New York's East Side. "How about votes for women?" called out the unscareable Maud Malone. "Madam," said Mr. Roosevelt, "I have asked that you women be allowed to vote to determine whether or not you shall vote." Just that; he never told whom he had asked, but the mere fact that he had asked was enough. All the women have to do now is to keep still and wait till somebody "allows" them to vote whether they want to vote. If one over one-half of the twenty-four millions says "yes," then they can all go right out and vote. But if one over one-half says "no," then the 11,999,999 that want to can't. Beautiful plan—so simple, so statesmanlike! But it seems to lack provision for a recall and a new deal.

Two women card sharps on a big ocean liner are said to have relieved a number of the male voyagers of all their ready cash. Another flagrant instance of woman's usurping an occupation that rightfully belongs to man!

Vice-President Marshall can't do anything for woman suffrage because his wife doesn't believe in it. That might be a sufficient excuse for Mr. Marshall as an individual but it is rather thin for the Vice-President of the United States.

"Bachelors are much more likely to become insane than married men," is the decision of the Massachusetts Mental Hygiene Conference. Yes, the mere fact that they choose to remain bachelors shows a mental twist.

A New York paper sagely remarks, "Under any system we shall not get a government of cherubs until we become cherubs ourselves." That's too long ahead. Men have always told women they were angels, so why not begin with woman suffrage as the first step?

"All the blessed creatures have to do," said Representative Adamson, of Georgia, in his speech, "is to intimate in a gentle way, in their charming tones and pleasing manner to the lords of creation that they wish to have the privilege of voting." How much that reminds one of Heflin, of Alabama—it's so different!

"Women of New Jersey," said ex-Assemblyman Matthews at the legislative hearing, "if you want to improve the conditions of public life, I beg you to keep on being women." As they felt that conditions very much needed improving, and for various other reasons, they adopted a resolution to keep on being women.

For the fourth year in succession a woman has won the prize of $1,250 offered by an English publishing house for the best first novel. It is bad enough that there are a million more women than men over there, without having them add to the offense by such performances as this. They'll never get the vote.

The president of the Pennsylvania Anti-Suffrage Society asks its members to "write to all the United States Senators, except those from the suffrage States, and tell them that the great, silent majority of women do not want the vote." She was very kind to omit those gentlemen—they might laugh themselves to death.

The Anti-Suffrage Association claims the credit for defeating the appointment of a Woman Suffrage Committee in the lower house of Congress. The only question voted on in the Democratic caucus was that "woman suffrage is a State and not a Federal question," but this will not disturb the complacence of the "antis." They will simply claim that they originated the doctrine of State's rights.

The Texas preacher who asked all the women of his congregation on Easter Sunday to take off their hats had St. Paul beaten to a frazzle.

The "antis" are failing to scare the suffragists by warning them that they will get the worst of it when they "rouse the brute force in men." As long as they are gradually getting everything they ask for they will never believe that men are brutes.

Englishmen are howling because, under the new income-tax law, the wife can find out how much property the husband has. But didn't she know already, as he promised at the altar, "With all my worldly goods I thee endow"?

There seems to be some anxiety lest the new women internes at Bellevue Hospital may not be able to jump on a speeding ambulance. Some encouragement is given by the news from Vassar that one girl has just thrown a basketball seventy-five feet and another has "smashed the broad-jump record" with a jump of over nine feet. Give the new internes a chance.

A man in the audience of State Senator Helen Robinson, of Colorado, called out that as there was only one woman and thirty-four men in the Senate, this showed it was a place for men. She answered that as there were eighty-seven women and eight hundred men in the State penitentiary, this evidently showed the same thing. Doesn't she know that men won't love her if she talks like that?

Why are there so many more widows than widowers? Because a man finds marriage such a nice institution that he gets right back into it, while a woman—well, she doesn't.

Ex-Speaker Cannon says that as women can now vote in Illinois it is a good time for handsome men to run for office, and that is why he ran. But Illinois women can't vote for Congressmen and that is why he was elected.

The women of Alaska, at the first election since they were enfranchised, elected an entire non-partisan ticket. It is no wonder the old party machines put on speed and try to run over a woman-suffrage amendment.

According to the latest medical discovery, love causes an intoxication of the nerve centers which may lead to insanity. That is probably why people who are in love are said to be crazy about each other—their nerve centers are on a spree. Cynics might call marriage a jag cure.

The anti-suffragists say that the suffrage movement is driving women away from marriage and "the feminist movement is turning marriage into a trade for alimony," and yet that the two movements are one and the same. But how can a woman make an alimony bargain if she has not been married? It really seems as if those "antis" had set out to prove the charge that the feminine mind is incapable of logic.

If the anti-suffragists would observe their Golden Rule, that "a woman's place is at home," it would not be half so easy for those other women to get the ballot.

Outside of the South only two States voted solidly against the woman suffrage amendment in the lower house of Congress—Vermont and Delaware. Please excuse them, they're such little ones.

Virginia suffragists have discovered that in 1829 her women petitioned a constitutional convention for the franchise. That was only eighty-six years ago, and petitions from women are seldom acted upon in so short a time as that.

At the legislative hearing in Massachusetts, the other day, one of the opponents said she did not believe women ought to vote but thought one-half the Legislature should be composed of women. Just as her sister "antis" always have done, she keeps one eye on the offices.

During the recent registration in San Francisco, automobiles were provided for the women, while the men were left to walk, and they rent the air with their protests. In Washington a jury composed of men and women had to go to the country to inspect some property. The women were sent in automobiles and the men in wagons, and their anger could be heard for miles. As the young woman wrote to her sweetheart, "The trubble with you is you are jellus."

Possibly women as well as men may be at their best when fifty, but they will never give anybody a chance to prove it on them.

Representative J. Hampton Moore, of Philadelphia, is quoted as saying it will be 20 years before Congress hears any more about prohibition or woman suffrage. That 0 must be a printer's mistake, and even the 2 is fifty per cent. too much.

Indiana women have formed a council to work with the Legislature "for the uplift of women and children." Wouldn't it be of greater benefit to the State if they would work for the uplift of the legislators?

Anti-suffragists are censuring Senator Helen Ring Robinson, of Colorado, because she is in the East lecturing instead of at home legislating. But she can't unless the Governor calls a special session, as the Legislature does not meet this year. Those anti-suffrage objections are such funny little boomerangs!

New Zealand has just been celebrating the twenty-first year of its equal-suffrage law. To be sure that country is some distance off, but it seems as if we should have heard of the wrecked homes, ruined families, declining birth rate, feminized men and general reign of socialism, polygamy and other things which the "antis" declare will follow woman suffrage. If they will then they have done it, so let us have a bill of particulars from New Zealand.

A Chicago lawyer secured a big alimony for his client on the argument that a man who marries a handsome woman must dress her in a style befitting her beauty. This ought to put the plain woman several laps ahead in the matrimonial race—but it won't.

If the colonel feels a little disheartened at the lapses in the Progressive party while he was away revising the map of South America, he can cheer up at the boom in votes for women. There will be more than twice as many of them in 1916 as when he set out to round them up two years ago.

The Supreme Court of the District of Columbia has decided that after a wife has left her husband's bed and board she may establish her own domicile wherever she pleases. That is an improvement on the old law, which did not allow her any place to sleep and eat legally without her husband's permission.

Mrs. John Martin, a leader of the "antis," said recently, in a public address in New York, "If they dare attempt to force the ballot on us here in the East, they will find that we are the daughters of the heroes who fought and bled at Concord and Lexington, who starved at Valley Forge!" Seems as if we had heard somewhere that those heroes did all that for the specific purpose of obtaining the ballot. "Descendants" is a very suitable word to apply to their daughters.

It was a woman who solved the "Million Dollar Mystery" and received the $10,000 prize; but that isn't the worst of it—she hasn't any husband to take care of the money for her.

The Anti-Suffrage Society forbids its members to say, "Woman suffrage is coming!" That's right—it shows a lack of originality to use the same slogan as the suffragists and how can they expect to raise money for a campaign against a sure thing?

A rich New Yorker, who has just died, left his fortune for his daughters in the hands of masculine executors because he doubted women's wisdom in business. How did he happen to have so much confidence in men's honesty in business?

Speaker Clark is no "neutral" when it comes to woman suffrage. During the House debate the other day the officers of the Suffrage Association were invited to occupy his bench in the gallery and have luncheon in his rooms at the Capitol. Give him the Iron Cross.

A man in Chicago has written a booklet against woman suffrage, in which he relates that when he was a small boy he and his sister were attacked by wolves, which his mother drove off with a gun. "If she had been a suffragette," he says, "she would probably have been away from home that night attending a political meeting and Sister Lucy and I would have been eaten alive." Sister Lucy might have been a loss to the world.

A wife has recently laughed herself to death at one of her husband's jokes. At least there is the consolation that she never will have to listen to any more of them.

The anti-suffragists say that "feminism and the family are inherently and irrevocably incompatible." When we find out what that means we are going to get mad about it.

Professor Hugo Münsterberg, of Harvard University, after years of careful research has decided that women form their opinions and judgments just as rapidly and accurately as men. Thanks for that small concession, kind sir! It is so unexpected!

The women anti-suffragists have just held their first convention, while the suffragists have had them by the hundreds. Now let the antis get up one parade and match it against the more than a thousand suffrage parades on May 2d, to prove that "the vast majority of women do not want to vote."

A speaker at the annual convention of the National Municipal Leagues takes President Wilson to task because his "History of the American People" scarcely mentions women. Why single out the President's for what is common to all histories? The women ought to get even by writing histories themselves and leaving out the men. That is almost though not quite the case in the history of woman suffrage, but the men are mentioned whenever they vote it down.

"The cause of equal suffrage is so one with civilization and humanity that I wonder any civilized man can be against it," is the latest utterance of William Dean Howells on the question. He was careful not to say "civilized woman," because he did not want to hurt the feelings of the Anti-Suffrage Association.

The president of the Arizona Federation of Women's Clubs said, in a recent speech, "It requires courage to be a good statesman and only nerve to be a good politician." To apply this formula to suffrage—it requires only nerve to be a good anti-suffragist, but one really has to wonder where they get enough of it.

A six-foot woman who has recently been appointed purser on a Hudson River boat is opposed to suffrage because she does not feel equal to the burden and she thinks it would tend to make women take men's jobs away from them. Her picture in the papers should be labeled "The Typical Anti-Suffragist, an Unconscious Humorist."

One member of the lower House of Congress obtained unanimous consent that another member's eulogy on his dog should be printed in the Congressional Record. Worse stuff probably has gone into that Record; but if two women members of the Legislature in some of those Western States had been guilty of this performance wouldn't the country have rung with their unfitness for office?

The reformers say that when woman is economically independent she will be free to do the "proposing." Perhaps then she won't want to.

A man has started to walk with a donkey from Maine to Oregon on an election bet. The photographers should label their pictures, "Find the man."

Great Britain has solved the race-suicide problem. Hereafter the parents, where either is insured, will get thirty shillings for each new baby. What a simple solution! What a magnificent recompense! The little island won't hold the infants.

The judge of the Chicago Domestic Relations Court gives six reasons for the trouble in married life, and one of them is the interference of mothers-in-law. If it were not for the other five reasons, there would probably not be so much necessity for mothers-in-law to interfere.

The Anti-Suffrage Association is very desirous of adopting a color for its very own, but thus far has found that all in the rainbow and out of it have been pre-empted by the innumerable suffrage societies. The "antis" over in England had just such a difficulty, but finally decided on blue and black. Then they had made a button and on it placed the head of a dear little chee-ild; but when the black and blue infant made its appearance, it was received by the suffragists with such screams of laughter and proffers of sympathy that it suddenly vanished and was never seen again.

In Denmark the men police are going on a strike, because the new women police are to have a higher salary than men get when they begin. There is nothing strange about this news, except that Denmark should pay women such salaries.

A woman office-holder who is getting a $4,500 salary says: "No, I am not a suffragist. Why should I want to vote? Men have always been mighty good to me." Prosperity sometimes does affect people that way—makes them so nearsighted they can't see what is happening to their neighbors.

There doesn't seem to be any particular reason why four or five women should have been guests of honor at the annual banquet of the Police Lieutenants' Benevolent Association, but they just sat up there and sang, "We're here because we're here." And that isn't the worst of it—they're going to be everywhere else and the men who don't like it will have to go to the edge of the earth and jump off.

The president of the New York Press Club in talking lately to a woman's society on suffrage said: "Keep within the sex line. I and the men behind me will never forgive you if you step outside of that line!" Is it anything like the bread line? And how are women to know if they fail to toe the mark exactly? They are as far now from what was originally considered the "sex line" as if it was the equator and they were at the poles and yet the men seem to have forgiven them.

If the New York women keep on rolling up that big suffrage fund the men will feel it their bounden duty to take over the management of the amendment campaign.

A New Jersey woman has been obliged to get a divorce because her husband was so "inordinately fond of dress" that he spent all his earnings on his clothes. Vanity and foolishness know no sex.

New York State has 101.2 men to every 100 women. That extra one and two-tenths of a man ought to make it entirely possible to give a vote to women without fear of changing the style of sex domination.

Some of the men are angry because the women said they are going to ride in the Washington suffrage parade with an imbecile, an insane person and a convict. The men say that the only time a woman should keep such company is on election day.

With an amendment for full suffrage pending in a certain State, the opponents believe in nipping any voting tendencies in the bud; so the district attorney announces that any woman giving a tea party to induce other women to come out and register for the school election, at which women can vote, will be prosecuted under the corrupt practices act. Of course then he will prosecute the ward bosses who round up the men in the back rooms of saloons to arrange for their registering and voting. Or is it only drinking tea that is a corrupt practice?

In Missouri there are 141 unmarried men to 100 unmarried women. It seems as if every woman there ought to be able to get a husband, but perhaps some of them are particular.

Some of those husbands who stay out late nights are surprised that the suffragists find it necessary to have so many classes for training inexperienced speakers.

Winston Churchill mispronounced a Greek word in the House of Commons lately, to the consternation of its members. Imagine the commotion in the House of Representatives at Washington if a member should make a mistake in his Greek!

"Our only problem now," says the national anti-suffrage president, "is, Can we make the negative majority large enough to keep the voters from having to vote on it again for twenty-five years?" No use to waste any time and money figuring on that problem. The answer is, It can't be done.

One of the New York Supreme Court justices, in adjourning a case against a woman recently, said, "My sex has been deceiving the other sex since the day of Adam." There has always been a suspicion that in that little transaction in the Garden of Eden it was Adam himself who was deceived. Since then possibly the men have been trying to get even, but it looks nowadays as if the women were beginning to claim their share from the tree of knowledge, and deceiving them was not quite so easy.

The only "perfect woman" has been found at Cornell University. To find perfect ladies visit a bargain counter.

A noted astrologer has seen in the stars victories for woman suffrage in many States. The "antis" see stars every time there is a new victory; but when they pick themselves up they never make any forecast of the future.

Cuban women are organizing for the suffrage and a flourishing society already exists in Hawaii. Truly the anti-suffragists are kept so busy these days trying to stem the tide they are obliged to forget that a woman's place is at home.

The candidates on the primary-election tickets in New York all had numbers opposite their names, so that voters who couldn't read or remember carried the numbers of their choice into the polling booth and copied them on the ballot. It almost seems as if women might have intelligence enough to perform a feat like that.

A tablet has been discovered in Babylonia, recording that the first world was created by a woman, and the male gods, growing tired of it, wiped it out by a flood and created another. There is a nice thing about this record—it has no account of Eve's eating the apple and bringing sin into the new creation. This removes one charge against woman and puts it up to man to account for the large amount of wickedness that has crept into his world.

That English anti-suffrage mother had no right to feel insulted when her "militant" daughter sent her a post-card with the one word "doormat" written on it. Wasn't it the English writer, Dinah Mulock, who said women ought to be satisfied to be doormats in their husband's home?

There seems to be some mild excitement over the question whether a woman should be allowed to write "Mrs." before her name when she is really "Miss." The chief effect would be on the men, who are much more chesty before the unmarried women that believe them to be heroes than before the married, who know they are not.

A Philadelphia clergyman says that "women's clubs are the instruments of the devil." With several million women enrolled in them, His Satanic Majesty should have a large working force; but it's odd that every one of them seems to be trying to improve something or somebody. Maybe the minister meant to say men's clubs.

The Business Women's League of Nashville, with three hundred members, has united with the Equal Suffrage League to move on the Legislature. Apparently they have never heard from the lady "antis" what a hindrance the ballot will be to the working woman but it is not yet too late for the "antis" to save her from "impending doom," in the classic language of their president.

The anti-suffrage women are boasting of the cooperation they receive from men. Sure—they are playing the game for the men!

Secretary Lane, of the Interior Department, says there will be no Indian man without the suffrage when he goes out of office. The surprising thing is that previous administrations have allowed a male of any sort to escape having it thrust upon him.

The wizard of Hoboken announces that the zodiacal sign of Sagittarius signifies that woman suffrage will be successful. Yes, all signs point that way; but is there anything in the zodiac to indicate when?

Why is it that as soon as women get the suffrage in any State they are called upon to clean up the cities and purify politics? As men have always been held to be so much better qualified to vote than women, the latter ought to find every city a Spotless Town and the political atmosphere too rarefied to breathe in safety.

The college girls all marry, according to recent statistics. They have to pass laws in many States to prevent school teachers from marrying. You can hardly keep a trained nurse single until her patient gets well. Stenographers go like hot cakes. The only girls that seem to have trouble in getting married are the old fashioned, womanly kind that do the sweetly domestic acts in the seclusion of the home.

At the big dinner given in New York for the Men and Religion Forward Movement the dean of Yale Theological School said: "The Church must have men because men are militant." Go to: isn't it militancy that is ruining the Women and Suffrage Forward Movement?

Ex-President Eliot, of Harvard, anti-suffragist, says, "Women are better adapted to work for the human beings of the future than men are." Yes, and as there wouldn't be any human beings of the future if it were not for women it almost seems as if they were of enough importance to have a vote.

Why should the advocates of woman suffrage be criticised for trying to defeat members of Congress who are opposed to it when all of the parties do their best to prevent the election of their opponents? If the suffragists did not try to keep their enemies out of Congress they wouldn't have political sense enough to vote.

The corporation counsel of the District of Columbia has ruled that the new eight-hour law for women applies to those who do mechanical work in a newspaper office, but not to those who do brain work. He probably considers that those big, forty-page papers are a greater strain on hands than brains, and it sure does seem like that when you try to read them.

"As for me, I defy you women. Come and meet me on the stump." Such were the brave words of a New York alderman, and from that moment Ajax defying the lightning was simply not in it.

All over the country ministers are giving sermons in favor of woman suffrage. Why don't the "antis" get some of them to preach against it? Surely a few can be found who would dare to do it!

Mrs. John Martin, opposed to a vote because it will turn women from matrimony, says that "soon the only women to marry will be the infirm and the idiotic." The anti-suffragists will continue to be eligible, won't they?

Ex-President Eliot has come to the front again to declare that there wasn't any Garden of Eden or Adam or Eve. All right. Then Eve didn't eat the apple and bring sin into the world; therefore that objection to giving the ballot to the women of the United States is null and void.

Just at the psychical moment when the *Alienist and Neurologist*, a St. Louis publication, devoted several pages to prove that the "cave man is the type women adore" and that "the bigger the brute, the more a woman clings to him," a New York wife took a 200-pound husband by the ear and led him to the police station, and one the same size in Chicago had his wife arrested for cruel and inhuman treatment. It looks as if the women themselves were trying the role of the cave man.

Have a Father's Day, by all means, if any of them feel slighted; but wouldn't a "night" be more appropriate?

They say that a stenographer is the only woman to whom a man can dictate these days. Is that the reason so many men marry their stenographers?

The New York suffragists are hunting for some means of moving Senators Root and O'Gorman to favor their amendment. They might try an earthquake.

The manager of a large school for the athletic training of girls says he has a number of pupils who can "heave a weight one hundred and eighty feet." It almost seems that if women can do that they ought to have the physical strength to heave a ballot into a box.

The anti-suffrage ladies mourned over the women's peace parade because it showed such a "thirst for publicity." Yes; those timid, shrinking creatures themselves wouldn't do a thing except parade up and down the streets wearing a big American Beauty rose to attract attention to their being "antis;" open headquarters in conspicuous places, call mass meetings and orate from the platform, besiege Congress and Legislatures, attend political conventions and go before the committees and send their representatives all over the country to conduct a publicity campaign against the suffragists. Oh, yes, they're "shrinking" all right—getting smaller every day.

"If women go into politics, who will do their work?" wail the "antis." The men can do it, as they've already taken most of it away from the home.

How could anybody wish the poor congressmen a Happy New Year when they had to begin it by voting on woman suffrage?

The churches and the social-uplift societies seem to have almost as much trouble in stopping the tango as the government does in putting an end to the snake dances among the Indians.

That new woman fire inspector in New York reported in one week thirty-seven violations of the law. The next thing she knows she will lose her job.

A hen at the Agricultural College of Oregon has laid 283 eggs this year, while the roosters stood around and crowed; and a cow in Michigan has given 18,733 pounds of milk, while the—but why specialize in order to prove the superior value of "the female of the species?"

Miss Julia Lathrop, head of the National Children's Bureau, says, "The anti-suffragists are like the hypnotized chickens which balk at a chalk line when there is nothing beyond." Yes, and after the ballot is actually given to women they are just like chickens when some corn is dropped the other side of the chalk line.

French annuity companies have discovered that women live twenty years longer than men, and now they propose to give women a choice of dying young or having their premiums raised.

"If my mother-in-law comes to heaven, I'll leave," wrote a New Orleans man, just before he committed suicide. Doubtless she will speed the parting guest.

It is too bad that members of the European nobility cannot come over here to hunt grizzly bears without being accused of seeking a rich wife, but perhaps it is because their graces and lordships have so long considered American heiresses as game.

Chicago women say that when they had to go to the City Hall before they got the ballot the officials there were polite but now they are cordial. In other words women without a vote are tolerated; with it, they are welcomed. Unfortunately many women don't know the difference.

Morrison I. Swift, lecturing on the "Humanist Forum," whatever that may be, says, "Women are amazingly incompetent to bring up children, have no special aptitude for it and it is doubtful whether they have any real liking for it." So? Well, perhaps men had better try their hand at it for a while; but any woman who ever left father in charge for a few hours and remembers the general chaos she found on her return has her doubts as to man's aptitude along this line.

"Woman's closer relation to the machinery of government is inexpedient," says the chairman of the New York anti-suffrage press committee. Well, if she takes out an accident policy she might run the risk of watching to see that it doesn't slip so many cogs.

An army of suffragists have just ended a 400-mile walk from Edinburgh to present a suffrage petition to Prime Minister Asquith. The suffragette way is quicker—they just wrap it around a stone and throw it through his window. Both branches of the movement seem to have proved that they possess the physical strength to cast a ballot.

The health commissioner of New York is determined that all the restaurants and hotel dining-rooms shall display signs telling how much benzoate of soda and similar stuff there is in the pastry. It is often asked why men make so much better cooks than women but no such signs were ever necessary on the pies that mother used to make.

Irvin Cobb told them at the Kentucky dinner that "the reason woman suffrage is not a success in his State is that woman can never be man's equal because she is always his superior." That remark has a sort of "befo' the wah" flavor. Women accept man's word that they are much his superior but when they get the ballot they will try to improve his status.

A "mere man" complains in a Chicago paper that "men have dwindled in importance in the eyes of women." Don't worry! They are just as important as ever in their own eyes.

The pugilists of California are so mad because prize fights are prohibited that they are going to move out of the State to spite the women who did it.

The Los Angeles woman police officer who is touring the Eastern States gives as one great advantage of woman suffrage that men no longer have to go down town to talk politics. A good many men would consider that an argument against it.

The secretary of state for New York is willing to concede a good deal to women, but insists on the "physical superiority" of men. Then how do all life insurance statistics happen to show that women live to a much greater age than men?

Dr. Forbes Ross, an eminent English physician, has discovered that in two thousand years the men will have degenerated into gorillas. The women can save the race, he says, but not if they insist on the vote. The women will probably answer that they will take the vote now and run the risk of the gorillas two thousand years hence. And, when one comes to think of it, after the treatment the suffragists in England have received from some of the present generation of men, gorillas would have no terrors for them!

Another English doctor heard from! This one deprecates the present style of dress because "it does away with the mystery in women, which is greatly against their own interests." Let the doctor calm himself—woman will always be enough of a mystery to keep the men busy guessing.

A Florida woman writes to the National Suffrage Association for permission to organize a troop of cavalry women, arm them with light rifles and send them to the Legislature to get a suffrage bill. The Southern women have been rather slow to get started but when they do they will go on horseback where the Northern women have gone on foot.

The chivalry of medieval times was of poor quality compared with the brand they have in Kansas. A man out there was too chivalrous to stand as candidate for an office when he found his opponent was a woman. This is a vast improvement on going to war with your lady's handkerchief on the point of your spear.

On the adjournment of Congress, when the men who had been fighting each other for months and using language that had to be expunged from the *Record* fell on one another's necks and wept and sang "Blest be the tie that binds"—it was then the women in the gallery realized that their sex is far too emotional and hysterical ever to make the laws for the nation.

Alexander Graham Bell says in his letter on eugenics, "Always remember that you are marrying a family, not a person." Alas, yes; and if you forget it you are very apt to be reminded of it afterward.

Now that President Wilson has received Colonel Harvey and Colonel Watterson with open arms he ought to be ready to do the Abraham act with the suffragists.

It cost $11.40 a piece to register voters in Greater New York for the spring election. Will those who are clamoring for a referendum of the suffrage question to women themselves at a special election please state who will foot the bill?

Dr. Mary Walker is greatly disgusted with the suffragists for making so much fuss to obtain a right which is already guaranteed to them under the Constitution. If she really believes this let her try to cast a vote at the next election. There is always room in jail for one more.

The Anti-Suffrage Association has issued "The Woman's Creed," which says, "I believe in making every effort to protect the good name of our American men from the attacks of the suffragists." Bless their soft, little hearts! One would think from their literator that the suffragists hadn't any men of their own that they would fight to the last ditch for if necessary. What the "antis" should do is to protect men from the blandishments of the suffragists after their votes.

As man has only fourteen pockets in his clothes the tailors are now putting in another, a secret one, where he can hide his money from his wife. As it is only the size of a watch pocket she won't grudge him the contents; besides she will know where it is located almost as soon as he does himself.

An "inspired" article says that there are signs of a revolt among the wives in nearly all the royal families of Europe and that "it is because the ideas of

Mrs. Pankhurst have permeated the circles of royalty." If Mrs. Pankhurst had accomplished no more than this, she would deserve all the honors her followers claim for her.

The president of a New York club said in her address to the City Federation the other day, "You neglect culture and buzz around too much; you should set aside ten minutes every day to meditate on something refining and ennobling." Like that speech, for instance; but isn't ten minutes a day an awful lot of time to spend on culture?

The 140,000 members of the Woman Suffrage Party in New York City are balloting for their officers in the different districts. The Anti-Suffrage State Society announces that it is increasing at the rate of one thousand a month. This proves that in one hundred and forty months it will catch up with the city party, provided the latter doesn't add any new members.

The most important thing in regard to the candidacy of that woman from Kansas who is running for Congress is that it shows there is no constitutional barrier to women members of Congress. All they have to do is to get elected.

The anti-feminists have always related with great joy that it is the female mosquito which does the biting, but scientists have now learned that the reason the male of the species refrains is because he has nothing to bite with.

At the next registration in Montana after women were enfranchised, there was a sprinting match to see who would be enrolled first; but sad to relate it was won by the two leaders of the anti-suffrage movement.

A fashion periodical offers a large salary to a young man who understands the entire subject of a woman's clothes and can edit a woman's magazine. As has been often remarked, women are invading men's domain and crowding them out of their legitimate work!

The first Anti-Suffrage Association in the United States or any other country was organized in Massachusetts in 1884. It has labored diligently ever since with the excellent result that both houses of the Legislature have voted by immense majorities to submit the question to the electors. If the "antis" will do their level best, it may pull through at the polls.

Dr. Hugh Cabot, of Puritan Boston, says that "if women want men to reform, they must cease to tempt them." Maybe so, the poor things! but how did they ever happen to be called "the stronger sex"?

The Guidon Anti-Suffrage Club of New York is devoting itself to a study of the Bible. Nobody needs the consolations of religion quite so much just now as the anti-suffragists.

That dull thud which was heard in the direction of Springfield, Ill., was Senator Shaw, of Decatur, being dropped from his committee chairmanships because he presented a resolution to repeal the woman suffrage law.

The wife of Congressman Taylor, of Colorado, says the women of that State have found that it does not take as long to vote as it does to match a piece of silk. It is to be hoped not or the worst fears of the "antis" as to the neglect of the home and family would be more than realized.

Sir Almoth Wright says that women ask for the suffrage because they "have not been taught the defects and limitations of the feminine mind." This is not because Sir A. W. and men of his stripe haven't wasted a good deal of more or less valuable time pointing them out; but in another chapter he says, "Failure to recognize that man is the master lies at the root of the suffrage movement," and to this the women plead guilty when they can stop laughing.

The French courts have decided that a married woman may spend as much on clothes as the rent of her home. If she lived in New York she could dress like the Queen of Sheba.

The big council of the Chippewas in Wisconsin recently declared for woman suffrage. The Indians know what it is to be without a vote; they are not like the chesty white men, who never did a thing to earn one and therefore don't want to share it.

A New York paper said, after the recent primary elections, that "the people seemed inflexibly determined not to rule." Before this statement is accepted give that half of the people a chance who have been trying to get it since 1848.

Miss Ida Tarbell says, "I don't take much interest in magazines for women only, as I am incapable of differentiating women from the human race." It is only when it comes to having the right of individual representation that Miss Tarbell would differentiate women from the rest of the human race.

At the anti-suffrage headquarters opened in Washington at the time of the parade they announced that during the first four days two thousand persons registered. Some of the suffrage mathematicians figured out that this would mean a registration of more than one person every minute for eight hours of every day—a manifest absurdity. It seems sometimes as if the sole object of the suffragists was to be disagreeable.

The Sir Almoth Wright who has recently written a book on woman suffrage which can't be mentioned in good society is the same individual who last year put forth a treatise against taking a bath; but really he should have allowed an exception after reading his book.

The "antis" say that when legislators favor woman suffrage because they think the women will vote for them, they forget the women who don't want it and will vote against them to get even. True, and they don't take into account what a tremendous power these women are already with their "indirect influence."

The egg crop is said to be worth as much to the country financially as the cotton crop and far more than the wheat crop, and women to be responsible for nine-tenths of the poultry crop. It might also be said that the hens are responsible for all of it but they don't belong to the sex that does the crowing.

What are the women coming to? A man jumps up in the midst of an eloquent speech by the president of the National Suffrage Association and asks her to marry him, and she answers that she would rather have a vote than a husband! The time was when a woman would rather have a husband; but then she never had had a chance to know the value of a vote.

According to the society notes our women will now have to wear gowns made by American dressmakers: All right; it doesn't matter who makes a woman's dress if only they will make enough of it.

Sensible women are terribly mortified sometimes as they look at the fashion illustrations in the Sunday papers, but when they turn to the next page and see the baseball pictures they feel that in the ridiculous women have been outclassed.

Mrs. Havelock Ellis, an English woman lecturing in this country, advises all women to refuse to kiss their husbands until they get the suffrage. This would be somewhat risky, as getting the suffrage is a slow process and meanwhile the husbands might go elsewhere for their kisses.

"Let us, oh, let us hold fast to monogamy!" wail the "antis." "Scientists believe it is the normal and natural relationship of humans." Then don't be alarmed, for even woman suffrage cannot entirely destroy what is natural and normal. One husband, one wife. All right. Now let every "anti" catch a husband—if she can.

The leader of the suffrage forces in Chicago says that "to appeal to American men's sense of justice is all women have to do in order to obtain fair dealing," and the Indianapolis *News* comments: "That's the way to get results—flatter the brutes!" Yes, the Michigan women recently tried it and they got results all right.

No, the public has been too thoroughly hardened by the present styles in women's dress to be frightened at anything that may happen if hoop skirts come in again.

Boston's new mayor has dismissed all the women employes from the office, on the ground that "it is not a fit place for women." Probably he knows what kind of a place it is going to be from now on.

In a temperance play running in New York the husband asks, "Where is my wandering wife tonight?" The answer of course should be, "At a suffrage meeting," for women never neglect their homes for any other purpose.

A good many people always seem to be in doubt, along at inauguration time, as to how the great Jefferson got up to the Capitol. It is to be hoped the gentleman himself knew whether he was afoot or on horseback on that auspicious occasion.

The anti-suffragists have issued a ton or so of literature to show that the constitution of women can never endure the nervous strain of voting. Now the presidents of the State medical associations in all the States where women have been voting from two to forty-five years have signed a statement that if anything has happened to their constitutions their family physicians haven't discovered it. The "antis" are playing in hard luck—every time they start out a nice little theory it runs up against a fact and is smashed to splinters.

Some time ago the women of Larned, Kan., met and resolved to use horsewhips on the professional gamblers if they did not leave the town. Now they have not exactly turned their spears into pruning hooks, but they have exchanged their horsewhips for ballots, and when they tell the gamblers to leave town they will gather up their outfit and go.

Some men are making an effort nowadays to scare women out of their independence by letting them stand in the street cars; but the women answer that they are better able to stand than many of the men they see sitting down, and that, according to statistics, a woman has a good many more years to ride on street cars than men have.

"We stand for an economic system which will enable every man to support a family so that women need not go outside the home to work," say the Socialists. A good idea; but suppose some men wouldn't use their earnings that way, and some women would rather work outside and support themselves than to do the same amount of work inside and have to be supported?

"The action of the Federation of Clubs at their biennial, indorsing woman suffrage," says Mrs. Dodge, national president of the "antis," "was a clear case of gag rule in a packed convention." Well, if the suffragists could "pack" a convention to the extent of ninety-eight per cent. and "gag" two thousand delegates they are certainly almost clever enough to vote.

The woman who recently climbed to the top of Harvard Glacier in Alaska is a strong suffragist. Seems as if it would have to be a cold day when she was not able to go to the polls.

New York's Alderman Quinn objects to woman suffrage because it would make monkeys of the men. Don't worry—a lot of them haven't waited for woman suffrage.

A young "efficiency expert" in Chicago tells his audiences that because a woman's heart is in matrimony she is and always will be a failure in business. Give her a chance, son! Business is a matter of the head.

Under the English poor law medicine cannot be supplied to a sick wife unless her husband makes application for it, and if he can't or won't support her the almshouse will not receive her unless he will come along. To understand the reason for the suffragette movement over there, read the laws.

Those clever antis! What wonderful research work they are doing! Having discovered that woman suffrage has led to polygamy in Wyoming, Colorado, Idaho, Washington, Oregon, California, Arizona, Kansas, Nevada, Montana and Illinois, they have now found, according to their official statement, that it means "the deliberate return to savagery." Alas, yes! one can hear the war whoops even now—they sound like the suffragists celebrating a victory!

Frenchmen often express great sympathy for the wife-ruled American husband, but they can't point to a case over here where wives have a quarrel and then stand their husbands up to fight a duel in order to settle it.

Congress treats women better than their forefathers did, for rather than pay taxes they destroyed the women's favorite beverage—tea—and held onto rum; but Congress has taxed beer and whiskey to the limit and left the women their soft drinks.

The New York *Tribune* congratulates the country that the American woman is not trying to be a man. The very idea! As if women, having almost reached the top step, would deliberately turn around and tumble to the bottom!

The-anti-suffragists have declared officially that they "recognize man as the head of the nation's household." All right, he is welcome to sit at the head of the table; but that doesn't mean that the rest of the family must not have anything to eat.

The Chicago *American* allows the women to get out a "suffrage" edition and they clean up a neat little profit of $15,000 for the "cause." The New York Hippodrome gives the suffragists a benefit performance and their treasury can't hold the profits. Seems as if we never hear of any anti-suffrage special editions or theater benefits. Wouldn't anybody buy or go?

All the pilots and captains on the Panama Canal are now required to be teetotalers. Pretty soon they will be forbidden to swear, and then Colonel Goethals will have to get women to run his boats.

President John Adams is said to have declared that "politics are the devil's own," but that was when "they" belonged entirely to the masculine half of the population.

A London physical-culture professor has announced that it is possible for every woman to have as perfect a figure as the Venus de Milo. If it is to be so common as that, the most of them would prefer to look like somebody else.

They do say that out in those Western States husband and wife frequently vote the same ticket to avoid discord in the family, but it is not always the ticket which the husband thought he was going to vote when they began discussing the matter.

A number of States have enacted a law that men who are physically unable to get to the polls may send their ballots by mail. This should dispose of the objection that the franchise must not be given to women because so much of the time they would not be well enough to go to the polling place. Incidentally, if men are not able to get to the polls, they are not able to fight, and therefore, if women must not be allowed to vote because they cannot fight, then these incapacitated men should be disfranchised.

The National Women's Anti-Suffrage Association announces that it spent less than $10,000 in the seven campaign States last fall. Why should it waste even that much good money when the other branches of the opposition were amply able to furnish hundreds of thousands and did so?

"Oh, suffragists, do you know that if you succeed the future men will be one-sided mongrels in nature and education, having had two fathers and no mother?" (Anti-suffrage document.) Good gracious! Just to think they've got 'em like that in those Western States, and the rest of the country doesn't even know it!

When the women of a certain church in Brooklyn ask for a voice in its affairs they are told that St. Paul commanded women to keep silent in the churches; but when they take up the calendar Sunday morning they find a request from the deacons to take off their hats. They are now insisting that Paul and the deacons come to an understanding.

Leaders of the anti-suffragists insist that women shall not be enfranchised against their protest, but when all the big organizations of women in the country are asking for it, who is making the protest? What is the matter with that ninety per cent. the antis claim to represent that they can't speak up? Ninety per cent. can make a great deal more noise than ten.

President Wilson said the last session of Congress accomplished so much simply by "sawing wood." He was careful not to add, "and saying nothing."

John Redmond and his followers want home rule for Ireland but they don't intend that those who rule the home shall have any part in it.

The entire State of Kansas is quarantined because of the foot-and-mouth disease. This is the strongest argument against woman suffrage that the "antis" have been able to find for a long time.

"Persons who try to stop the woman suffrage movement," said a Chicago elections commissioner, "are in the position of a man throwing himself in front of a locomotive." Well, they always expect that the bosses who run the political machines will apply the brake.

The latest government report from New Zealand, where women have voted twenty-one years, shows that, while the population has doubled in thirty years, the number of men in prison has increased only from 631 to 853, and the number of women prisoners has decreased from 94 to 64. It seems from these figures that woman suffrage in New Zealand did not double the criminal vote and did not produce a reign of anarchy and crime. Perhaps it is only in the United States and in those of the States where it has never been tried that it will have this effect. Still the "antis" should bolster up their charge with a statistic or two.

The Keith and Proctor circuits forbid any burlesquing of the suffragists. That's right, and the anti-suffragists give their own continuous vaudeville performances.

One little woman in the big Woolworth Building in New York manages the electrical apparatus for running twenty-eight elevators—and yet some people think a woman hasn't nerve enough to drop a ballot in a box.

Gertrude Atherton says, "Women politicians will be just like men politicians—no better, no worse." We knew, of course, that they couldn't be any—well, we had hoped they might prove to be a little better.

"Young women," said Representative Bowdle, of Cincinnati, in the suffrage debate, "will beware of this movement, which positively destroys all feminine charm and deters young men from marriage." (Loud applause by the sixty-seven married members from the twelve States where women vote.)

Before and after taking was strikingly illustrated by the Missouri Legislature in its action on the woman-suffrage amendment. The senate adjourned to the assembly chamber to hear the women present their case. The committee reported unanimously in favor. Both houses adopted the report by large majorities. Then St. Louis suddenly got busy and the Legislature rescinded its action! It heard its master's voice!

By a new law voters in Nebraska can send their ballots through the mail when necessary. This answers the question, Who will care for the baby when mother votes? Mother will and Uncle Sam will deposit her ballot. Anti-suffs knocked out again!

The doctors are now admonishing the women that if they keep on with the present style of tight-fitting hats and headbands nothing can save them from baldness. Women have been listening to this kind of prophecy for several generations and yet have kept their hair on; but when they look about they observe that nearly all the men are baldheaded.

Representatives of nearly all the organizations of women in Chicago are demanding that places shall be given to women on the boards of education, of parks and of libraries. How can they do it when they see how splendidly all matters connected with the municipality are managed by men? Women don't seem to be showing that old-time admiration and trust which used to be their greatest charm.

The Simple Life and Open Air Exposition in London is exhibiting the Fully Furnished Man, who carries on his person all the necessities of life except food. That is nothing to be proud of. All the other animals have done this ever since they ceased to belong to the vegetable kingdom. The only difficulty will be to keep this new kind of man out of civilized society.

Why try to get acquainted with the people on Mars, when we have so little time to give to those we know on earth?

It is charged that 46,000 men have deserted from the regular army during the last ten years. Should women who are willing to fight but can't be disfranchised on that account, while men who can fight but won't are freely granted the vote?

One of the Western railroads has placed a woman in charge of its dining car and the customary howl at women's usurping the work of men is now in order. To be sure having charge of a dining-room has always been considered a woman's business but that was only when there was no salary attached.

"We must abolish everything that bears even the semblance of privilege," is the Wilson slogan. Thanks, Mr. President. Will you kindly get yourself into a state of mind where you can see that the possession of the suffrage by only one-half the people is about the most iniquitous privilege that could exist?

Mrs. Dodge, president of the Anti-Suffrage Association, wants to go into the fight against suffrage in the next presidential campaign with 500,000 women at her back. All right; she will need every one of them. But what is to become of the half-million families while the wives and mothers are marching on to victory behind Mrs. Dodge?

"Bustles" for women are to be the fashion this spring. Thanks for the prospect of even that much relief to the helpless onlookers.

Mr. Croker's Indian bride says she cannot be a "squaw" until she is a mother. Oh, yes; first a squall then a squaw.

"The pay here," said Mayor Curley, of Boston, in dismissing all the women in his office, "is quite sufficient to maintain a man." Then how on earth did women ever happen to get the jobs?

"Behind the skirts of suffragism," says an official statement of the "antis," "Mormonism goes to the polls, socialism marches red and rampant on the streets, and feminism stalks and swaggers in our homes." The old-fashioned thing—to wear skirts so wide as all that!

The Alimony Club of divorced husbands in New York are howling loud and long because the court has ruled that they must continue the payment of alimony even though they are kept in prison and can't earn a dollar. Another crowd who are out of jail are rending the air because they have to pay alimony just the same after their former spouses have wedded again. The fair divorcees answer that since only men are considered competent to make the laws or even to elect the lawmakers, they have no right to kick against the results. Its awful the little respect women show nowadays for the superior wisdom of men!

It is rather late in the day to warn women against being "jostled at the polls." That is about the only place where they would not get jostled.

Paris is tired of the tango. Public opinion caused it to be danced too respectably. It may hold on awhile in the United States, we can stand a considerable amount of respectability, but not too much when it becomes unfashionable.

No, Ethelyn, Lu Lu Temple is not the name of a woman suffrage headquarters. It is the rendezvous of an ancient and honorable body of men in Philadelphia, where they think women are too frivolous to vote.

Arkansas has now been added to the list of "dry" States by action of its Legislature and Wisconsin requires a health certificate from would-be bridegrooms. No woman suffrage in either State. Really the men are getting so good nowadays there will be nobody for women to reform when they obtain the ballot.

The superintendent of public schools in Cincinnati will start "a six months' course of study for prospective brides," and besides all the usual housekeeping stunts they will be taught to calk a water pipe, put up shelves, mend door knobs, etc. If he isn't careful he will create a prospect that will scare all the girls away from matrimony. Women can be so many things nowadays besides carpenters and plumbers.

The New York *Tribune* says, "Another ten years and the clinging vine will be only a moist and tender memory." What a fortunate thing for the oak!

The sphygmograph is the invention of a woman doctor and the person who wears it cannot tell a lie, even to his wife. Something of this sort was bound to happen when women were permitted to enter the medical profession.

"Feminism is the process of putting father out of business," is a specimen anti-suffrage epigram. If feminism means that able-bodied young women shall earn their own living, perhaps father will have a chance to get something ahead for his old age.

The Reno *Gazette* in its fight against the suffrage amendment said that when a straw vote of the women was taken in 1895 in Massachusetts, they declared against enfranchisement 38 to 1. Suppose they did—what has that to do with the women of Nevada in 1914? The fact is, however, that the women voted in favor of it 25 to 1. Next!

And so the anti-suffrage ladies are going into the thick of the congressional fray to help elect the men who will promise not to give them a vote! It is now in order for them to get up a street parade and then the suffragists won't have a thing on them—they will have done everything they were afraid they might have to do if enfranchised and they haven't got the ballot as a compensation for doing it. The joke is on them.

The ancient question, "Could women voters work out their road tax?" has been answered by two in Iowa. They did worse, for they won two out of three prizes offered by the county for work on highways. It was all right for them to do the work but very wrong for them to win the prizes.

"Women never could serve on the police force," an anti-suffragist rushes into print to declare. "Could frail woman withstand, year in and year out, the severe climatic changes constantly occurring?" Well, several million of her do, as they start out each morning to earn their daily bread.

The "antis" are dreadfully vexed at the suffragists because of their reported attempts to convert the women public-school teachers, the women in the government departments, the women wage-earners and women in divers other capacities. Putting it mildly they are like the schoolboy who wrote, "To sum up Daniel Webster's character—it is one which I do not approve!"

Some awful things are promised in the season's styles for man. They are to be more expensive, which will require him to owe his tailor more than ever. Evening trousers are to be very loose so that he can perpetrate the tango and turkey trot without accident. For the rest of the day the clothes are to be very tight so as to show the natural form, and this is where the public will start a suffragette movement.

Do not criticise Mr. Bryan because he said nothing new in regard to woman suffrage. Everything that could be said was said long ago but until recently the political ears were very deaf and very long.

In Chicago, before the women took a hand, the disposal of the garbage cost the city $4,000 a month; now it nets a profit of $2,000 a month, and yet people wonder why the grafters are so dead set against votes for women.

The various parties seem to be having a hard time with the "political uplift." Some day it will occur to them that until women lend a hand they will be trying to lift themselves by their bootstraps.

They opened a big hotel in Los Angeles a few months ago for men only, and already they announce that henceforth women also will be welcomed as patrons. Funny, isn't it, when hotels for women only are flourishing all over the country, that the men couldn't flock alone in a single one?

Before the last committee hearing on woman suffrage in Washington, Mrs. Dodge, national president of the "antis," announced that the members of Congress had been sufficiently bored, so to speak, and her forces would not appear. The love of the limelight was too strong, however, and there they were in the center of the stage, singing the old, sweet song, "Woman's place is at home in the bosom of her family."

The turkey trot and bunny hug have been replaced by the goose waddle, which is really much more indicative of those who dance it.

"Love is a disease," says a Chicago doctor, "called anaphylaxis—lack of resistance." This is merely a trick of the profession to increase the number of their patients, but the Chicago girls dare them to try to cure it.

A booth was built in New York City in a district where only three men voted, yet members of the Legislature object to giving suffrage to women because it would require more voting booths. Who helps to pay for those the men use?

The anti-suffragists have been so busy during the campaign running political headquarters and making speeches for the candidates they haven't had a minute to tell the suffragists that a woman's place is at home and that women are wholly unfitted for politics. It will be somewhat embarrassing for them to resume business at the old stand and hear the suffragists jeer.

When United States Senator Burton, of Ohio, landed from a trip to Europe not long ago and was asked the inevitable question about woman suffrage, he said, "I do not care even to express an opinion on such a subordinate issue." Now he says that of course he is going to vote for it in his State. It is taking a mean advantage for reporters to corral a great statesman on the dock before he finds out what has happened in his absence.

The Rothchilds are said to have given $15,000 to the British Anti-Suffrage Association. The vote in the hands of women would prove a strong factor in preventing the wars of the future.

Colonel Henry Watterson declares that he has "written more times and at greater length against woman suffrage than any other editor." Maybe he has and maybe that is the reason it is making such rapid progress in his own State.

California University girls eat ten tons of candy a year, according to reports; but the boys of that institution can't prove that they are the sweetest things on earth until candy statistics from the other colleges come in.

Women's place is at home. Wives must make the home so attractive that husbands will never want to go out evenings. Children must be kept off the street. All very good; but how is the whole family to stay at home at the same time in a city flat of the average size?

The moving-picture shows are making a specialty of films depicting the newly enfranchised women of the Western States in the act of going to the polls and voting, but strange to say there is not a single illustration of the awful things that were going to happen when this catastrophe took place. It seems odd that after the terrible predictions of fifty years the scene should look much like a procession going to church—except that there are more men in it.

"How To Be 'Smart' Though Middle-aged" is the title of an article that is going the rounds. The smartest thing the middle-aged can do is to recognize that they are middle-aged and act accordingly, and this applies to men as well as women.

No woman nowadays makes the promise to obey in the marriage service with the slightest intention of keeping it, so why compel her to prevaricate to the minister? Let her reserve that privilege to use with her husband.

The courts of Missouri have decided that a husband cannot be arrested for burning up his wife's clothes, as they are his, not hers; but after his wife learned of this decision the man soon found himself in jail for disturbing the peace.

"Man is the natural protector of woman," shouted several thousand of the species as they attacked the suffrage parade in Washington. "Man is the natural protector of woman," echoed the policemen as they turned their backs.

The "antis" ask why the suffragists are not afraid to trust men with the musket in time of war, but are afraid to trust them with the ballot? Bless you, nobody wants to take the ballot away from them; but the suffragists can't see how a man can represent more than one person with one ballot, and, besides, some of them haven't got any man, and they think it isn't fair to be deprived of both the man and the vote.

Recently, at an anti-suffrage meeting in one of those wonderfully progressive towns for which Connecticut is noted, forty ladies signed a remonstrance against giving other women something which this immortal forty did not want for themselves. Where was Ali Baba with his oil can?

When the women watched that crowd of men in Madison Square Garden cheer and howl and whoop and yell an hour and a half for one candidate, and the next night a similar crowd go through the same performance the same length of time for another candidate, they fully realized that women are too emotional for political life.

A great editor criticises the Washington suffragists severely because they reserved so many rooms for the out-of-town paraders that the inaugural committee couldn't find enough for its marchers. "They lost a great opportunity to win the new administration by unselfishness and sacrifice," he said, and the women haven't quit laughing yet.

The president of the Woman's Club at Boise, Idaho, where they have had equal suffrage for nearly twenty years, says that "nothing puts the fear of God into the hearts of men like the ballot in the hands of women." Yes, a certain class of men feel much more comfortable to know that women are using the beautiful, indirect influence of prayers and tears.

Sir Almoth Wright says the advocates of equal pay for women do not know the commercial value of having the employe work shoulder to shoulder with the employer. Yes? No? What about the good-looking stenographer?

The President of France is considering the proposal to decorate with the Cross of the Legion of Honor the mother of twenty-two children. Something that could be exchanged for twenty-two pairs of shoes would be more appropriate.

Seven girl students of Leland Stanford University have just been elected to Phi Beta Kappa and not one of the boys, although they outnumber the girls two to one. Comment would be impolite, not to say unfeeling.

New York women have announced that the day for women's "auxiliaries" is past, and Chicago women have given notice to the men of that city that they will not serve on any more "sub" committees. Really, that Declaration of Independence of 1776 begins to seem like rather a weak document.

Perish the thought that a minister of the Gospel—and especially a woman—should contest with a horse race! But when the Rev. Anna Shaw, president of the National Suffrage Association, began speaking from an automobile behind the grand-stand at the Wisconsin State Fair, the whole crowd climbed down to hear her and forgot all about the races.

First fruits of woman suffrage! A San Francisco wife has just been granted a divorce because her husband talked too much!

Dr. Mary Walker advises girls to put on trousers. They might not be so pretty but they would certainly be more modest than those things women are now wearing.

The scientific world is highly excited over the report of the birth of an atom. Its chief interest to women is the effect it will have on their getting the suffrage, as the public insists on connecting this in some way with the birth rate.

The Buffalo *Express*, commenting on the public schools teaching boys to sew, says: "Quite necessary! For how will the women of the future get their gowns, if men do not learn to sew?" They can get them just as they do now—from the male dressmakers who got onto the woman's job as soon as there was any money in it.

Women have a good deal to learn about politics. There was the woman candidate for mayor of San Diego, who announced that her first act if elected would be to put through an ordinance taxing bachelors. Naturally the bachelors all voted against her; the benedicts did the same because they didn't want the bachelors to feel that there was such an easy escape from marriage, and the women turned her down because they thought she was quite capable of levying a tax on spinsters.

The public has borne with some fortitude the close-fitting garb of women—it has had its compensations; but now that the National Association of Clothing Designers has decreed that men's clothes also must be tight fitting—well, if the police fail to do their duty the common people must rise up.

The Supreme Court of Illinois has decided that the women of that State may vote for President but not for county commissioners. If they had a choice, they would much prefer to vote for the commissioners, whose work comes a great deal nearer home to them; but the party "bosses" would rather trust them to vote for President as there is no local graft in that office.

The national anti-suffrage president says, "The extent to which suffrage agitation detracts from charitable enterprises is appalling." How can this be when that lady herself assures us that the suffragists represent less than ten per cent. of the women? Ninety per cent. surely ought to be sufficient to do the charitable work, if they can spare the time from chasing after the suffragists.

Some men are organizing a pneumatic-tube system through which from a central kitchen hot meals can be shot to any part of the city day or night. Women sometimes wonder whether men intend to leave them any domestic duties. About the only thing untouched is the nursery, but a man has invented an electric cradle that rocks itself, so woman will have to find some other way to move the world.

A Kansas City judge has ruled that under certain circumstances wives may lie to their husbands. The latter never waited for any judicial decision.

From the fuss made about Dr. Anna Shaw's shaking her fist during a suffrage speech one would think it was the size of a sledgehammer, while really it is about as big as a little red apple.

A record has been unearthed in London, showing that women used to be plumbers in 1500. Very likely; but that was before the business became so profitable that only men were competent to engage in it.

The manager of the largest vaudeville circuit in the country has issued orders that there must be no more jokes at the expense of the woman-suffrage movement. Lovers of humor need not be discouraged, however, for the literary bureau of the Anti-Suffrage Association will still continue to issue its bulletins.

Dr. Geisel, president of Shorter College, Georgia, says that institutions of higher education interfere with women's natural destiny. Chancellor Day, of Syracuse University, says if college women don't marry it is because their marriage standard is higher and they are not finding men fitted for fatherhood. As all the colleges can't be abolished in order to lower women's ideal of marriage, it looks as if something will have to be done to bring men up to the new standard.

Husband applied for a divorce because his wife was "absolutely independent." Judge granted it and he started off to find a dear little dependent who would give him a sort of manly feeling.

King Alfonso is said to have become an advocate of woman's rights under the influence of his British Queen. Can't she be spared long enough to go home and try her hand on Cousin George?

Young and impecunious members of the nobility may now be rented out for afternoon tea in London. This is not a bad use to make of them, but they could command a higher price in New York and Washington.

Is one reason why so many men oppose woman suffrage because they are afraid their wives would obey St. Paul's injunction to ask of their husbands at home when they wanted information and questions on political issues might prove embarrassing?

At the suffrage hearing before the Massachusetts Legislature the "antis" evidently got their Irish up, as Molly Maguire called equal suffrage "the most deadly menace that ever faced the State," and Joseph Murphy said, "I am one of a family of fourteen children and my mother didn't need any vote to do it." Perhaps it wouldn't have been safe, as she was such a "repeater;" but Pa Murphy's chest must have swelled with pride when he went to the polls on election morning and represented sixteen people with one ballot.

"The Silent Woman," an ancient play, has been resurrected, perhaps as a reminder of something gone forever. The anti-suffragists used to claim that title, but if they are not making as much noise as the suffragists nowadays it is only because there are not nearly so many of them.

At the recent election in Louisiana the men voted down a constitutional amendment to allow women to serve on school and charity boards, and the election officers in New Orleans were so afraid it might slip through that seventeen were indicted for "padding" the returns against it. Doubtless they intended this simply as an act of chivalry.

Governor Marshall, of Indiana, said recently to the Council of Women in Indianapolis, "There is not a working woman in this city doing an honest work who is not more important to this State than the Governor." Funny he should talk like that when the women there can't vote; but he only confirmed the suspicions they had had for some time.

The Anti-Suffrage Association sends out a press bulletin saying, "We object to being called away from uplifting the world through the old channels of education and religion to assist in uplifting it by the doubtful channels of the ballot box." They need not leave their job for it is such a big one that if derricks are erected in both channels it will still be necessary to call for outside help.

Prime Minister Asquith is caricatured by *Punch* as Mona Lisa with the smile that won't come off. To the suffragists he looks more like the cat that swallowed the canary.

"The clinging-vine type of women will continue to multiply," we are assured by those who claim to know. Well, that is a very good business, since they don't seem to be able to do anything else.

In all the New York public-school gymnasiums the number of girls exceeds the number of boys. This does not indicate that the girls are preparing to be militant suffragists but only that the boys would rather smoke cigarettes and shoot craps.

Secretary of State Bryan says he wouldn't feel sure of the support of women as they did not vote for him when he was a candidate; but he must remember that he hadn't discovered then that he was in favor of woman suffrage.

Admiral Chadwick's recent assertion that "women teachers develop in boys a feminized, emotional, illogical manhood" is receiving some support from great editors. It is very peculiar that mothers have always been taught that their finest work is to train their boys for the highest duties of citizenship, and yet if these same boys spend a few hours each day in school with women teachers they are ruined for life. Is it only when there is a salary attached that a woman's teaching becomes dangerous?

That ancient skull found in England proves conclusively, so the anthropologists say, that man had reason before he spoke. Well, well! What a revolution has taken place since those prehistoric days!

A Paris jeweler has invented a ring to be worn by the divorced—two marriage rings intertwined in the form of a cross. Very inappropriate, when the wearers have just laid down their cross.

A Russian woman has just started to explore an Arabian desert of thousands of miles, which no European has ever entered. How thankful she should be that the heavy burden of casting a ballot has not been imposed on her!

The first thing the women of Oregon did with their brand-new ballots was to cast them against letting foreigners vote on their "first papers," which they had always done. Did somebody remark that women are too radical to be trusted with the suffrage?

A Baptist minister in Chicago has opened in his church a school of home training to make women more desirable for wives. That school had better be closed by the authorities for women are so "desirable" already that school boards, theater managers, telegraph and telephone heads, even the government, are requiring those they employ to guarantee that they will not marry within a specified time. A school to make women less desirable—that is the need of the hour.

A Cincinnati legislator has introduced a bill for a commission to "prescribe the fashions to be worn by women in the State of Ohio." One good thing about it would be that when it came to appointing officials to enforce the rules not an office-seeker in the State would be left without a job.

New York's commissioner of corrections suggests that the one hundred and seventy-five wife beaters on Blackwell's Island be put to making creosoted paving blocks. Good idea! The perfume will remind them of what awaits them after their exit from this world of inadequate punishment.

That Englishman who was put into jail because he had no money to pay the taxes on his wife's property must have a poor opinion of the law-making ability of his sex. Women couldn't do any worse, unless they condemned the poor husband to death.

The Norwegian Parliament first gave municipal suffrage to women taxpayers; then gave them the Parliamentary franchise; then it removed the taxpaying qualification for the municipal vote. Its next step was to make them eligible for all political offices. Then it granted them the right to speak in the State church, but would not allow them to preach; now it proposes to let them hold the Church offices. Lastly it gave the complete franchise to all women. There are only a few more inches to cut off and the State is bearing up as well as could be expected.

The young men of Cairo who have returned from European universities have begun a crusade to "emancipate" the Moslem women from the veil. Let us believe they are wholly disinterested.

A woman who kept a grocery wanted to decorate her show windows in the anti-suffrage colors but she had no American Beauty roses, so she put in a lot of red lobsters. To make it still more appropriate she should have added some clams.

The English government has just raised the pay of the men clerks in the post-offices and reduced the pay of the women clerks to half that received by the men. To be sure hatchets are no argument but sometimes they express people's feelings better than logic.

"Since the Prince of Wales left his mother," say the press dispatches, "he has become a 'man' in the best sense of the word. He drives his car beyond the speed limit and is rarely seen without a pipe in his mouth." How fine! It shows that he is rapidly developing the qualities necessary for a great ruler.

Seven men in one precinct in a Kansas town had to get the election officers to mark their ballots, and all voted against the woman-suffrage amendment. Those officials were still more obliging in some of the Michigan towns, it is said, for they gathered up all the ballots that were left over and voted them against this amendment.

The anti-suffragists opened their campaign at Sherry's, in New York, the other day; but this does not necessarily imply that they used a corkscrew.

In many places the liquor sellers are complaining that the moving-picture shows, where a man can take his wife and children for five or ten cents, are ruining their business. Anything that keeps a man with his family is an enemy to the saloon.

The latest census report shows that there are about thirty thousand more divorced women than men in the United States. This seems to indicate that the men get back into the married state as quickly as possible but the women know when they have had enough.

The wild outcry of the anti-suffragists against "feminism" indicates that they prefer masculinism for women. Let them have it, for luckily they are not of enough importance for all womankind to be judged by what they do and say, as is the case with the suffragists.

The California papers congratulate the State that, "whereas it was in a ferment of suffrage meetings two years ago, now there is not the slightest turmoil but all is peace." This should be a lesson to other States where the turmoil is getting worse every day and there is just about as much peace in sight as there is in Europe.

Help, help! The pastor of the First Spiritual Church in Worcester, Mass., has to appeal to the police for protection from "lovesick maidens and scheming mothers." He'd better go West, where there is not such a scarcity of men and women can be more particular.

People used to object to letting women vote because of the publicity it would give them; but nowadays when one sees the public stunts of the suffragists trying to get the ballot and of the "antis" trying to prevent it, he devoutly wishes that they might all be made voters at once so they could retire to the privacy of their homes and families.

That big New York hotel that had to change its dainty, esthetic liquor buffet for women into a common bar for men, because the women would not patronize it, seems to prove two things; first, that the stories of the drink habit among women are greatly exaggerated; and, second, that it's always safe to start another bar for men.

The Anti-Suffrage Society of Washington passed at vote of censure on the Young Women's Christian Association of that city because it allowed the delegation of working women who called on the President to have a paid-for luncheon in its headquarters. The members of the association felt so badly about it that they immediately proceeded to give a circus.

South Carolina has employed three policewomen. Well, if the men insist on electing an individual like Cole Blease for Governor, it's up to the women to protect the State.

The new Socialist member of Congress says he will try to have a law passed that no workingman shall marry a wage-earning woman who has not a union card. Wouldn't a marriage certificate be a union card?

"For six thousand years men have been trying to run the world," said Speaker Clark, "and some people think they have made a bad mess of it." If it had been for only that brief space of time women might be willing to let them keep on trying awhile longer.

The favorite newspaper paragraph now in referring to the cheap suffrage-parade hats assures women that if they will wear forty-eight-cent hats all the year round they can have anything they want. Well, the first thing they want is for men to set the example by wearing hats at the same price.

The Denver police records show that married men are far more law-abiding than unmarried, and the New York City superintendent of schools says the married women teachers are much more amenable to discipline than the spinsters. There seems to be no doubt that marriage is the best known means of saving grace for the unregenerate.

They say that gymnasium statistics show a steady increase in the size of women's waists. In that case something should be done to bring about a steady increase in the length of men's arms.

The anti-suffragists are having a good deal of fun because the papers tell of a California mayor who does the family washing. Maybe he runs a laundry. Men are doing most of the family washings nowadays.

Andre de Fouquieres, who has come over from Paris to teach American men how to dress by lecturing at afternoon teas, says, "New York is the finishing touch of the world." Glad it looks that way. So many seem to come over for the purpose of making a finishing touch.

An eminent London scientist asserts that the points which distinguish the human race from the beasts are more marked in woman than in man. "For instance," he says, "her ear is more human than a man's." Maybe so; certainly she doesn't so often show the length of it.

The Fathers' and Mothers' Club of one of the Eastern cities farthest along in the science of eugenics has issued instructions to young men contemplating matrimony to study the mother, as the daughter is likely to be an exact copy. Suppose a girl is advised to study the father on the same principle—won't that put an end to marriage?

Now the suffrage societies of Canada have united in a National Franchise Association and Great Britain will soon have another lot of daughters who can outvote their mother.

Congress is considering a bill to give the suffrage to the men of Porto Rico. Can it be that there are any males under the jurisdiction of the United States without a vote? Shelve all other measures before Congress until this terrible wrong has been righted!

The women who have been running for office in those Western States have drawn the line on kissing babies, saying that they are too well versed in hygiene to commit that crime. As has been remarked, women are entirely too much given to sentiment to be allowed to vote.

Anti-suffrage literature declares that the enfranchisement of women will "efface the natural differentiation of function between the two sexes." Oh, no, it won't! Nature can't be effaced and the differentiation will go right on differentiating just the same.

What a queer way they have in Great Britain of encouraging matrimony! There are about a million more women than men, but when the Canadian government begged that some of the women might be sent over as wives for the English immigrants, the authorities in England vetoed it because the women were needed to work in the cotton mills.

Perhaps in the U.S. women should not vote because they cannot fight but the man in England who said this would have to run to cover.

"We believe that political equality will deprive us of special privileges hitherto accorded us by law," cry the anti-suffragists. How very sad! Will they please name one or two special privileges that the women have lost in those States where they can vote?

The government is closing all the saloons on the reservations to protect the Indians, and the Southern Legislatures are passing drastic temperance laws to protect the negroes. It seems to be left to the women to demand measures for the protection of the white men.

A Missouri legislator has introduced a bill that the buttons on the back of a woman's dress shall be as large as a silver quarter. Some time when those women legislators out West cannot find anything else to do they will introduce a bill that men shall cease wearing any buttons at all on the back and cuffs of their coat.

The Anti-Suffrage Association is to be congratulated on the latest contribution to its literature by Abdul Hamid, the deposed Sultan of Turkey. There is such a similarity between his opinions on woman suffrage and Mrs. Humphry Ward's that it certainly is either a case of plagiarism or two souls with but a single thought.

Harvard University has taken off the ban and allowed a speech on woman suffrage within its sacred walls. If the ban had remained on a little longer it would not have been necessary to take it off.

Almost the last words of Baroness von Suttner before she sailed for home were that there never would be peace here until the women had a vote. The men could have told her that as soon as she landed in the United States.

For many days before Easter, the dispatches said, the Cleveland suffragists trimmed hats to be sold for the "cause." Go to! It would be utterly impossible for a woman to believe in suffrage and know how to trim a hat.

Kansas women say that they have long been accustomed to masculine chivalry, as they have had the municipal vote for a quarter of a century; but since they got the full suffrage they are so overwhelmed with attentions from the men that they can hardly resist a political flirtation.

Strange, isn't it, how Government offices, public schools and the rest penalize matrimony, and then when women ask for the suffrage the opponents shriek aloud that it will destroy the desire for marriage? Doesn't it ever occur to them that the loss of all these business opportunities might have this effect? Husbands are nice, but oh, you salary!

Beatrice Harraden learned at a recent legislative hearing in Westminster that "the women impressed the statesmen but the statesmen did not in the least impress the women." We have always seen this in our country but we never let the "statesmen" know it.

The belated action of the New York anti-suffragists, in opening their little headquarters on Fifth Avenue a few days before the big suffrage parade "to offset any impression it might make," recalls the careful housewife, who exclaimed when she saw Niagara Falls, "Oh, that reminds me—I left the kitchen faucet running!"

It is perfectly proper for mothers of wealth and social position to employ nurses and governesses for their children; but when a business or professional woman does the same, society at large goes into hysterics over her poor, neglected offspring. If the mother is off playing bridge and attending "teas," it is all right; but if she is away earning a salary it is all wrong.

When women wanted to be customs inspectors the authorities said they could never, never climb the ladder on the side of a ship. Strange to say the two women who demonstrated that it could easily be done were both daughters of Presidents. It is odd how many obstacles can be placed in the way when a woman wants a job with a salary attached!

Amherst College is to establish a chair of common sense. Great pity that college isn't co-educational!

"When women are elected to Congress, there will be no more secret caucuses," says a great daily. Since when have there been any of that kind?

School inspectors in Russia have issued an order that no married woman teacher can have more than two children. They have heard about the New York board of education and gone them two better.

"Suffrage was begotten in Utah and Idaho by Mormonism," says a syndicate article sent forth by the Pennsylvania "anti" association. Oh, no; it was "begotten" in Wyoming, when there wasn't a Mormon in the Territory.

His name is Abnel—a German doctor who has made a discovery. "The world's well-being is threatened by the adoration of suffragists for dissolute men. The clinging, domestic women are naturally attracted to strong men." Of course—the men would have to be strong to support their weight. "But the women politicians have lost the selective instinct," he says. "They flutter toward the Don Juans like moths and are consumed before they realize their own folly." Yes, people notice this in those Western States—a perfect holocaust as soon as women get the ballot. That is why the Don Juans always vote against it—they would feel so dreadfully helpless with all the women politicians fluttering toward them in order to be consumed.

Which is likely to do more damage to the sweetly feminine character—to stand at the polls all day and hand out coffee to voters, or to deposit a ballot and then go home and attend to woman's legitimate business?

A cardinal in Venice denounced the tight skirts women are wearing and ordered them to do penance. They hastened to church the next day for the purpose, but were obliged to perform their devotions standing!

The New Thought devotees have thought out a new kind of marriage—"a mating of harmonious vibrations." But that has been the trouble with marriage in late years—the parties have vibrated among too many people.

A Chicago suffrage club has just been formed, to which only young, unmarried women are eligible. It seems only yesterday that girls were solemnly admonished that if they advocated woman suffrage no man would marry them, but they can't be scared that way now.

Richard Le Gallienne has gone Omar Khayyam's "a loaf of bread, a jug of wine and thou, singing in the wilderness underneath a bough," one better. He will be perfectly satisfied "if only she and I can go, walking forever through the snow." Maybe he would, but we think the lady would want something warmer even than Richard's poetry.

There was an increase of fifteen per cent. in marriages in Chicago the first six months after the Legislature granted woman suffrage. That may not have been the cause but if the figures had gone the other way there would have had to be a special session to repeal it.

The New York *Times* suggests that "the suffragists have the right of petition and by exercising it in a proper manner they may advance their cause." They have been doing this for sixty-five years. If there is any new style in petitions they will be very thankful for a diagram and a paper pattern.

Anti-suffragists are protesting against having that vote for suffrage at the biennial called unanimous. All right; say that twenty-one hundred votes were cast, and seventy of them were negative—thirty in favor to one opposed—and that is just about the way the woman's vote would stand throughout the country.

Pittsburgh is to have a saloon exclusively for women, as they have been crowded out of the others by the men. Promoters of the new idea should go to New York and inquire at the Hotel Vanderbilt, which started out with a beautiful "bar" for women, but a month later it was closed for lack of patronage and reopened as a much needed annex to the large and flourishing bar for men.

Prof. Spencer Baldwin, of Boston University, is an anti-suffragist. He doesn't like the new woman—"androgynous hybrid," that is what he calls her. It's up to the professor to find an anti-toxin.

In the United States the women say they won't pay their taxes if they can't vote and in London they say they won't pay their rent. Our government can compromise with them by giving the suffrage but what is their landlord to do?

The head of the "vocational bureau" in Boston thinks the time may come when graduation certificates in fathercraft and mothercraft will be issued by the public schools. But if the holders don't get aboard the matrimonial craft what good will these do?

Hampton Court has been closed to the public for a long time through fear of the suffragettes; but the government has at last evolved a scheme—it will open the palace and charge a shilling admission! How clever! But suppose a suffragette should be able to borrow a shilling?

Woman suffragists campaigning in Wisconsin came across a man whose wife has supported the family for years by walking the tight rope, and he announced that he should vote against the suffrage amendment because a woman's place is at home. There are a vast number just like him there, judging from the election returns.

Under a woman school superintendent in Rowan County, Kentucky, the number of illiterates in two years has been reduced from 1,152 to 23, and these are physically incompetent. One of the great dangers of equal suffrage is that women might aspire to hold office!

The women of Nevada have been holding a "sacrifice week" to raise money for their suffrage campaign, as also have women in the neighboring States to help them. By the way, can anybody recall any special sacrifice to earn the right that has been made by the men who are now doing the voting in the United States?

A Johns Hopkins professor says that in twenty years' experience with over a thousand graduates of both sexes he has failed to discover the inferior brains of women which he hears so much about. He should apply to the anti-suffragists, who not only can tell him all about them but can furnish him with plenty of specimens.

Secretary Daniels declares that "bachelors are encumberers of the earth" and offers the use of the United States navy to scatter their ranks. As the most of them are land animals the services of the War Department would be more effective. Meanwhile it is safe to say that few bachelors pass the age of fifty without the inner consciousness that they ought to be blown up or sent to the bottom of the sea.

At the next election after California women were enfranchised, the vote of the State increased 313,883. As has often been remarked, women wouldn't use the suffrage if they had it.

"The men are to put on their clothes with a shoe horn," is the latest fashion edict. We shall not believe it till we see it, and even then we shall look the other way.

Some "bootleggers" who are to be tried before a jury of women in Colorado are said to be feeling very anxious. Why so? The objection to women as judges and jurors has always been that they are too sentimental and emotional to mete out justice.

The illogical minds of women cannot comprehend why it is, when a congressman's constituents indicate that they don't want him to represent them in the government any longer, that same government immediately puts him on the pay roll in another place.

The male editors of the two leading fashion magazines are using columns of space in argument whether the women of this country shall adopt American or French styles. The National Association of Master Bakers, at their recent convention, adopted a resolution in favor of woman suffrage, giving as a reason that if women go into politics they won't have time to stay at home and bake bread. It is really outrageous the way women are crowding into the fields of labor that belong to men!

"It is a wise child that knows its own father," but in France they have just passed a law which will permit the mother to make some inquiries.

The new invention of making rubber tires out of a substance extracted from whiskey suggests that it would be an excellent thing on most of the "joy" rides if the whiskey was in the tires instead of the automobile.

The public-school teachers who want the suffrage have raised the cry, "Can disfranchised teachers train citizens?" Of course they can, so long as they can be had for half the price that a man would charge for the job.

A Democratic candidate for congressman-at-large in Illinois, who is an anti-suffragist, is making his canvass on the platform: "A husband and a home for every woman." As over twenty-five hundred husbands in Chicago alone last year abandoned their wives, he should add another plank that if he is elected all husbands will stick to home and family.

Just as the Anti-Suffrage Association issued its bulletin announcing that there was no favorable movement in the South, the Georgia Federation of Labor strongly indorsed the suffragists and the Atlanta *Constitution* declared editorially, "Success seems about to crown their efforts." The antis are playing in hard luck; no sooner do they get their type all nicely set up than the other side does something or other that knocks it into "pi."

One of those gifted male lecturers who know everything says, "We have new models of automobiles every year; we should work out new models of the antiquated family machine." Go ahead; women have no objection as long as they are permitted to sit at the steering wheel.

"Marse Henry" Watterson says he has found only three classes of women who want the suffrage: "Those who wish to exploit their own interests, those who are soured on life and the brainless sheep who think it is fashionable." Maybe it is like that in Kentucky, but the men in some States have found several other kinds.

The "bachelor tax" which the Montana legislators want to impose varies from $2.50 to $100 per annum, but the majority think $5 would be about right. It seems like cruelty to animals to put on any tax at all when there are more than twice as many men as women over twenty-one years old in the State and those across the border are in just as bad a fix.

Emile Deschamps tells us in his new book that the American woman cannot keep her husband's love because she does not return it. But if she returned it of course she couldn't keep it. Funny how many things these foreigners find out about American women never discovered by American men, who seem to be well enough satisfied not to go wife hunting in any other country.

Almost every organization in the "campaign" States which stands for anything that ought to be stood for has indorsed the suffrage amendment. Will the antis name one which has declared against it—that is, has declared publicly?

It's funny how every woman who does anything nowadays, from climbing a steeple to taking the prize at a beauty show, is described as "a leading suffragist." Don't the "antis" ever get married or die or have triplets or do anything worth notice?

One striking difference between the United States Senate and the British House of Commons is that when a deputation of women suffragists make a call the Senators receive them with open arms and the Commoners shout for the police.

The nurses who cared for Mr. Roosevelt in the Chicago hospital have been so deluged with offers of marriage they have had to go into seclusion. It's such a very funny way men have of showing their appreciation of a woman by offering to marry her!

The women in China, it is said, have now advanced so far that they are held accountable for their crimes instead of their male relatives. Here, too. It used to be the law in many of our States that a wife could not be punished for a crime committed in the presence of her husband. Having a husband was considered sufficient punishment for her—or at least that seemed to be just as good a reason as any for the law.

Captain Amundson, the antarctic discoverer, who comes from Norway where women vote, says of the English suffragettes: "They are quite right, and I'd like to help them in their fight for freedom." The captain had better confine himself to easy jobs like finding the South Pole.

The anti-suffrage headquarters in Trenton, N. J., have a big placard in the window, asking, "Why the Increase in Juvenile Crime in Denver?" Because, according to the chief of police, "juvenile crime in Denver has decreased nearly two hundred per cent. in the last ten years"—that's why. It is amazing how the anti-suffragists manage to acquire so much misinformation.

In Colonel Roosevelt's latest pronunciamento on the question of suffrage, he says that he "always believed it exactly as much the right of women as men, but he only favored it 'tepidly' until his association with such women as Jane Addams," etc. Is the colonel quite sure that he was not slightly influenced by those 2,000,000 women out West with the vote already in their hands?

At the recent suffrage debate in Congress a great deal was said about women "trailing their skirts in the mire of politics" by some of the befo'-the-wah members. Evidently the old gentlemen hadn't learned that trailing skirts went out of fashion years ago and now the men can't make the political mud deep enough to touch the hem of the up-to-date dresses.

The "antis" appeal to the legislators to "listen to logic instead of the dropping of ballots." Impossible! Compared with the thud of those ballots all other noises sound like utter silence.

Grand opera was sung to fourteen lions at the zoo in Berlin and they didn't do any violence to the singers. Audiences in many countries have been just as forbearing.

A society has been organized in New York to arouse in fathers more interest in their children. Perhaps they have already sufficient interest but in many cases it has to be spread out over such a large surface.

Miss Dora Keen, the Pennsylvania woman who recently climbed to the top of Harvard Glacier in Alaska believes that she has the physical strength to cast a ballot, but the men of her State insist that she must stay at home and let them protect her from being jostled at the polls.

All sorts of explanations have been made as to why those Kansas women, when they found they had won the suffrage, built a bonfire and threw their old hats in it. Perhaps they concluded that, now they were voters, they must act as silly as men. Maybe they had such swelled heads that the hats wouldn't fit. Possibly they thought they could get new ones on election bets. But most likely they only wanted to show that now their hats are in the ring and they are ready for the fray.

The *Woman's Journal* says the devil and the anti-suffragists will be busy all summer. Why both?

Now 12,000 bakers are going on a strike. It didn't used to be that way when the nation's wives and mothers baked the bread.

A National Desertion Bureau has been incorporated to try to settle all the domestic quarrels in the country. There won't be enough of that bureau left to kindle a fire on a marriage altar.

"Women must not have the suffrage," says an authorized document of the antis, "because Max Eastman's wife goes by her maiden name." Where does she "go?" That is much more to the point, if she is to decide the question.

"On one side," says a Pennsylvania official in the Anti-Suffrage Association, "are the mother and the home; on the other the woman seeking the place man occupies as the framer of constitutions and the administrator of civil-government." Seems as if we know of several men who don't frame constitutions or administer any kind of government, and a good many women who can't stay on the side of the home because they have to go out and earn the money to have a home. Men and women can't be divided like goats and sheep, and if they could, there is no valid reason why the voting booths should all be on one side of the line.

There is a great cry in Washington about retiring the superannuated clerks for the good of the service. What is impairing the service is the large number of inefficient chiefs of departments who are drawing big salaries while their poorly paid women assistants do the work.

For the second time a Radcliffe girl has won the $100 prize open to students of all colleges for the best essay on municipal government. Oh, yes, women may be very good on the theory, but only men have the practical knowledge. Just observe what a shining success they have made of city governments!

The way women will lose the respect of men when they get a vote was illustrated in Arizona, where as soon as women were enfranchised the men nominated the president of the Suffrage Association for State senator, and she received six hundred more votes than any other candidate on the ticket.

Votes for Women says that the Peers, when they argued against woman suffrage, should have been clothed in skins with feathers in their hair, and Lord Curzon, when he moved the rejection of the bill, should have begun by dancing around the woolsack and singing an incantation. We must protest against this libel on the American Indian; he would scorn to take an Englishman's attitude against the rights of women.

The State of Washington has the lowest death rate of any in the country; New Hampshire the highest. Moral—Go West, where women vote.

There have been but four "champion" typewriters, and three of these were women. As soon as the machine was invented women were at the keyboard, and yet you hear men operators complaining that women have "usurped" their positions!

When that International Congress of Women Voters meets in San Francisco next summer, there will be a fine chance to observe how the suffrage has unsexed women and destroyed the feminine instincts in at least nine countries.

Whenever anybody issues the edict that women have not the physical strength to vote some of them immediately shin up a flagpole on a fifty-story building and take a header off the Brooklyn Bridge for a moving-picture show, loop the loop in an airship and climb the highest mountain in the world.

Civil Service Commissioner McIlhenny says the women government employes may march in the suffrage parade as individuals but not as clerks. Thanks Mr. Commissioner! That is what the suffragists are asking for—to be considered as individuals instead of belonging to somebody or something. But they can't join a suffrage club, he says. As the man in prison answered his lawyer who said, "They can't put you in jail for that"—"They already hev."

An anti-Tammany bureau of a thousand speakers is being organized in New York to talk the "tiger" to death. Right there is where they need the help of women.

Medical statistics from Paris announce that men show most brilliancy from forty to fifty-six. This holds out a great deal of hope for a lot of men we know who are under forty.

"There is no reform legislation in any suffrage State which is not duplicated in those where women cannot vote," says the "antis." If that is so they will have to find some other excuse for beating the suffragists to the polls as soon as they get a chance.

The United States Senate has made an appropriation to erect a splendid memorial in Washington in recognition of the service rendered by women during the Civil War. By all means; and then don't deny the franchise to women because they cannot serve their country in time of war.

The Women's Political Association of Australia has called upon its national Parliament to protect the political rights of the women of that country, who become disfranchised the moment they take up a residence in any other part of the British empire, while men continue to vote. Here, too! Help for the women voters of twelve States, who, when they go to live in any of the other thirty-six, are reduced to the political level of the idiots, insane and criminal.

Shall women propose? Well, they have a good deal of nerve nowadays, but hardly enough to say to a man, "Please take me and support me for the rest of my life!" They must first be financially independent and then somehow they seem to lose interest in the matter.

When Utah's electoral college met to cast the vote of the State for President and Vice-President, its members selected the one woman elector to carry the result to Washington. Those Western States are constantly giving just such examples as this of the way men lose respect for women when they can vote and hold office.

In all of the Eastern cities thousands of children are kept out of school because there are no seats for them. Does any one believe this would be the case if women handled the school funds? A good many useless officials who are now holding down chairs would stand up and the school children would have seats.

Another English woman heard from! "American men," she says, "are arrogant snobs, who think they are the salt of the earth." That is a much more alluring description than to call them spiritless creatures, entirely dominated by women—the usual English idea. Whatever they are, they suit American women and the English women can't have them.

Mayor Mitchel ought to take it out on the powers that advised him to do it. How was one so young to know that a gun could have such a powerful back action?

Kansas suffragists declare they are not going to ask men for a penny to carry on their campaign. Maybe not but husbands had better go to bed with their clothes on.

A woman who has just returned to earth after a trance reports that she saw some male angels but they had no wings. Possibly they had at one time but found them inconvenient and passed them on to women, just as here on earth they did with skirts.

"Do women realize," says a writer in an anti-suffrage paper, "that as they become self-supporting they deprive men of the right to support them?" Don't worry; men can always find women who are willing to be supported—some of them find too many.

The National Women's Trade Unions' League and its various State auxiliaries and all kinds of working women's organizations are continually passing resolutions for woman suffrage. On the other hand, Dr. Katharine Bement Davis, superintendent of the Bedford Reformatory for Women, says that her charges, almost to a woman, are opposed to it. If a person is to be judged by the company she keeps, one hardly feels like getting acquainted with the members of the Anti-Suffrage Association.

It's all right for the Kansas Legislature to have a woman sergeant-at-arms, but it seems that her name ought not to be "Effie." By the way what does the sergeant have to do with her arms.

In the States where women can vote they have not exactly turned their swords into plowshares but they have transformed their suffrage societies into civic clubs, and instead of their begging men to give them votes, the men are begging women for the votes they already hold in their lily-white hands.

The Legislature of Alaska enfranchised women and then enacted a statute declaring that "all laws which impose or recognize civil disability on a wife that do not exist as to the husband are hereby repealed." As the "antis" are fond of saying, "Women must accept the suffrage at a terrible sacrifice of the privileges they have enjoyed."

History repeats itself. The Ceres Ladies' Society, fifty years old—the society, not the ladies—admitted a few men as a compliment and now has filed an ouster against them because they usurped all the offices. Sixty years ago Susan B. Anthony and Elizabeth Cady Stanton formed a women's temperance society and were persuaded to admit men, who at the first election, got control of the offices. The two women walked out of the society and out of the temperance movement straight into that for woman suffrage. Men should have a care!

They say that such a crop of eels never has been known. It's always like that during the season of candidates.

According to the decision of the New York board of education, no woman is fitted to teach children after she has had a child herself. Masculine logic!

The latest scientific discovery is that on the right kind of food a hen will lay a hundred per cent. more eggs. If she does the rooster will crow himself to death.

The papers have given wide publicity to the Arkansas farmer who offers a large porker to any one that will find him a wife. There is often an exchange of that kind in marriage, and the wife gets it.

The "antis" have announced that in their New York headquarters they "will overcome the yelling of the suffragists with exquisite music on the harp and other stringed instruments." At the same time the Illinois hospital for the insane announces an arrangement to cure their patients with music. There must have been collusion between the two. The methods and talk of the antis for a long time have indicated that they thought they were dealing with the feeble-minded if not the dangerously insane. The experiments will be watched with interest but the antis should hurry up, as the number of suffragists at large is rapidly increasing and it will require a lot of music.